BETWEEN DUST AND WIND

BETWEEN DUST AND WIND

Christopher Carter

RESOURCE *Publications* • Eugene, Oregon

BETWEEN DUST AND WIND

Resource Publications
An Imprint of Wipf and Stock Publishers
199 W. 8th Ave., Suite 3
Eugene, OR 97401

www.wipfandstock.com

PAPERBACK ISBN: 979-8-3852-1133-3
HARDCOVER ISBN: 979-8-3852-1134-0
EBOOK ISBN: 979-8-3852-1135-7

03/12/24

Contents

Preface

Rediscovering Poetry

It was late July 2022. The westering sun hued the air with grace-
ful golds. Wrapped in twilight gilding, I gingerly composed my
first poem in several years. Up to this point, I had adhered to rigid
structure: three stanzas composed of six lines. The first and third
lines, like the second and fourth, rhymed with each other. The
final two formed a couplet closing out the verse. But this time, I
eschewed the rhymes and sought to eject the structure. Instead, I
simply wrote as I felt led to in the moment.

This freedom to explore new poetic structures arose from a struc-
tured season in my life. In May 2022, I realized that some of the
depression symptoms that I struggle with were linked to inconsis-
tent fitness, diet, and sleep rhythms. So I started going to the gym,
running, planning my meals, and sticking to a bedtime pattern.

This routine quickly overflowed into the rest of my life. Instead of
haphazardly selecting books to read, pictures to take, and subjects
to write about, I crafted larger goals for my life and based my daily
routines around them. That regular schedule offered me space and
freedom to take risks with my poetry.

I tasked myself with writing one poem a day. Each one was crafted
in the way that resonated most with me in that moment. The first
poem, "before", was born on July 28, 2022. This work became a

catalyst for 30 additional entries I would pen over the following year.

While I knew a book was the end goal, I didn't know what the overarching structure would be. The daily writing practice, however, soon yielded an idea. I found myself writing poems based on simple biblical themes: creation, sin, hope, redemption, the human-God relationship, and so on. I spun that trend into a tapestry that recounted the story of Christianity. This narrative can be summed in the following pattern: creation, fall, incarnation (God becoming human in Jesus), redemption, and final restoration.

In my own life, poetry first found me on the outset of depression. In that mental state, I believed a fallacious narrative about myself. But as I engaged poetry more, God used it as a pathway to my heart, and he steadily disclosed the more fundamental reality, the way he saw me: his beloved. God often works through poetry.

Poetry as Truth-teller

The Bible narrative is the archetype that undergirds all other tales; its story plots perfectly onto the human psyche and gives structure to our existence. I saw this clearly as I penned my poems. Given this circumstance, it's no surprise that much of Scripture is communicated as poetry. The literary genre contains great power to both instruct and transform.

First, poetry is an effective way to instruct because it enables deep learning. Not only does it connect the reader and the writer with something they don't know, but it also does so in a memorable way. While prose conveys information practically, poetry travels the circuitous route. To some, the twists and turns in language are off-putting. But for others, the journey is precisely what makes the information easier to retain.

But poetry doesn't just deliver facts. It also communicates transformative reality. The main job of this artform is to disclose or bring out something that is obscured or unseen. It is a way of drawing out the truth and displaying reality as it is. This is seen in the Greek word for truth, *aletheia*. This word is a combination of the prefix -*a* and *lanthano*, "to escape a person's notice, be hidden, unnoticed, or cause to forget." Truth, then, is something no longer unknown, hidden, unnoticed, or forgotten. It is a person, object, or idea being known for what it truly is.

As poetry works to draw out the hidden realities of life, it does so by striving to touch the intangible and speak the ineffable. The artform isn't bound by the strict rules of proposition, so it has more freedom to give words to the wordless mystery of God. Though it will never define and delineate transcendence, poetry leaves us with the certainty there is a mystery to be known and pursued.

Poetry certainly had this effect on me. As I was emerging from struggles with depression and building healthy daily rhythms, I came into closer contact with a reality saturated by mystery. That encounter, however, was a process of slow transformation. Daily I patiently had to work with my new routines. Going on a single run wouldn't shed pounds of body weight, nor would reading 10 pages of a book make me a scholar. But the accumulated repetition of these small acts would lead me closer to the healthy person I envisioned.

So I invite you to pick up this book and read just one poem per day. Turn off your phone, shut your computer, and read in a quiet space. After you read the poem, spend three minutes in prayer contemplating the words you just met. I fervently hope that, as a result, these poems will help you in your own transformation process.

Acknowledgements

I find the "by" line of a book to be a bit reductionistic. It seems to say that all the words and thoughts expressed on these pages are the sole output of a lone individual with a laptop. The truth, however, is far more communal. So many individuals played a role in shaping this book. From moral support to manuscript review, *Between Dust and Wind* owes a huge debt of gratitude to the multitude of people who poured into this initiative. For me, this section is the true "by" line of this book.

I have to begin with a word of thanks to Mal and Madeline Maloney, the two friends who created a space that bore this book. Inspiration first hit me on July 4, 2022 as I overlooked the glistening waters of Lake Chelan in eastern Washington state. Ever since I moved to Los Angeles in 2021, I've made frequent trips to visit Mal and Madeline. Each visit was like a retreat where they would remind me how loved and valued I am. During one particular visit in July 2022, our conversations about making the most of life propelled me to cultivate my love of poetry.

As I was writing the individual poems, I read several famous poets for inspiration. Though these individuals have passed, I owe them a debt of gratitude. Without C.S. Lewis, J.R.R. Tolkien, T.S. Eliot, George MacDonald, Rainer Marie Rilke, and George Herbert these poems would be amorphous thoughts still swimming in my head. Thank you for helping me find the words to convey what lingered in my heart.

ACKNOWLEDGEMENTS

When I completed the manuscript in June 2023, I sent it off to several individuals for review. First, I am grateful for Anthony Miguel Cantu for doing the initial read-through of the book. His notes set me on the path toward the final product. Additionally, I am thankful for Lisa Cooper and the thorough review she provided. She is responsible for helping each poem to find its final form and for helping me find a consistent rhythm for capitalizing words at the beginning of lines. To James O'Reilly and the team behind *The Broken Binnacle*, I appreciate you publishing "sight" in your newsletter.

And finally, I owe a debt of gratitude to Brev Moss for helping me tighten the ideas behind each poem. We spent hours at a small pub in Santa Monica reviewing each entry. The conversation that came from those moments made me feel like I had found the start of my own Inklings. Each session left me more inspired than the last and deepened my joy for the Maker who inspires every good artistic pursuit.

To the individuals who provided endorsements for this book, I am greatly indebted. Dr. Esther Meek, not only were your ideas formative for me in the classroom, but they continued to stay with me as I wrote each poem.

To my parents who spent time reading my poems, sharing them on Facebook, and praying for this work, I am deeply grateful.

before

Before spark-struck stars,
burning like beacons,
signaled light to quiet worlds,
telling them it's time to spring life
upon barren surfaces—

before wind swept into
birds' lungs, breathing broad,
sweet songs, calling for companions
and praising the light gifted from
suns in distant galaxies,

before dust-fashioned man
walked the surface sprouting with life
and soaked in the light of celestial signal fires
and breathed in concert with winged choir...

before all beginnings began,
when stars were unstruck flame,
and breath was breeze unstirred,
and man was image unmade,
You were.

where

When I formed
formless earth,
where were You?

Before all things,
when the world was still,
at Your side I stood.

When I shut the sea,
and bounded waters,
where did You reside?

Over chaos
and crossing currents
we rested, together.

Who sings the solo,
distinct from
starry song and angel choir?

When day followed
Your command,
I was the Word letting it be.

sight

Like sunlight
dappling and
speckling
a forest canopy,
You dance and
move
between leaves,
Your face,
my first light,
my first sight.

Like a supernova
bursting and
spreading,
eternity swims
in Your eyes,
a gift foretelling
all the beauty to come,
Your love,
my best light,
my best sight.

Like a child
swaddled and
beheld,
I behold Your gaze,
longing and
burning
to see Your dancing light
and bursting eternity
always looking back,
my endless vision,
my only light,
my only sight.

law

Lines and laws,
laws and lines.
Do and don't,
don't and do.

Path to life,
road to death.
A fruit that can't be unbitten,
tracks of grace pursuing.

reward

Enjoy the sun—
Money amassed,
Health secured,
Foes downtrodden—
Bask in this life's wealth.

Sit under the cloud—
Dollars lost,
Disease diagnosed,
Enemies victorious—

Remember.

serve

Two masters
—You say—
No man can serve.

One you'll pursue,
his weight,
hard and heavy.

Another you'll avoid,
His yoke,
gentle and light.

His rest
will raise
the burdened man.

But his promise
will end
in broken backs.

Two masters
—You say—
one life, the other death.

eat

Take, see.
Isn't it a pleasant color?

Taste, eat.
Is God good to you?

Bite, chew.
Could the forbidden be so supple?

Savor, swallow.
What is that flavor to you?

nothing

A picture,
shaped
by positive
and
negative,
things present,
things absent.

Your images,
composed
of art
and
breath,
love given,
love given.

Yet

Our lives,
framed
by hoarding
and
hoarding,
false wealth
against void.

Empty pictures,
Cluttered
frames, images
speaking,
while
saying

nothing.

groan

Hear my prayer.

In the garden
gold-tinged sky,
wisping winds,
and animal cry
heralded Your presence.

In the garden
hope had sight,
prayer dripped like rain,
heaven strolled with earth,
God with his glory.

I am withered like grass.

In the desert
heat-scorched sky,
infernal winds,
and scavengers' wings
tease of absence.

In the desert
faith weeps for the unseen,
words wither as if unheard,
love smolders to ash,
man cleft from maker.

Let my cry come unto thee.

name

Between daffodil and poppy
we used to stroll,
lovers set
on fire by heaven's hearth.

like flower's fragrance,
Your name
wafted
from my lips,

but

like autumn leaves turning,
my love
withered
on the branch.

Between desert and bramble,
I walk alone.
Penitent, praying
for a name in a bush set aflame.

friend

Where you go I will go,
under Eden's boughs,
we walked.
beneath her vines,
I slept,
When You, my friend,
made a woman
from borrowed bone.
And where you stay I will stay.

Your people will be my people,
the fruit
catching my eye,
the snake,
charming her heart,
the curse,
sundering lover from beloved.
And your God, my God.

Where you die,
our lives wither,
our beauty wilts,
our bones are dried,
but Your Word never fades.
I will die.

wave

Deep to deep,
all of me,
for
all of You
yearns

but

Tied
down by
fear,
rolling like
waves.

Tired
of the
burden,
pulling like
gravity.

yet

Your waves
over me
crash.

Your breakers
plunge me
deep.

still

Tied and tumbling,
help me
trust Your
tide.

Elijah

Memories
shout and dance.
Disappointment
cuts and pierces.
Mount Carmel,
their victory, they claim.

Today,
as a seven-soaked altar.
Present,
a saturated wood pile.
Absent,
the one who makes this day burn.

Soaked
in grief,
Saturated
in loss—

is today
a funeral pyre,

or

is it
a holy fire?

son

On my back lay the wood,
In father's arms, knife and fire,
Though I knew our endeavor good,
I saw no gift for the pyre.
I asked, "Where is the lamb?"
"He will come from our I AM."

So we went to Moriah's mount,
Thick with thickets and thorns,
Yet for the offering I couldn't account.
Still on father went, like one who mourns.
His tears fell as quiet rain,
He with nameless pain.

Father set the stones,
and the wood he laid.
He trembled to his very bones,
Bearing what he would not say.
Then my hands he bound,
And laid me where offering wasn't found.

On the boards I was placed,
Laid on the wood I had to bear.
I, the promised one once embraced,
Was given like a criminal to his share.
I was made the sheep,
The lamb father couldn't keep.

Yet I heard bleating from the thorns,
A ram caught in the vine.
Father gripped it by the horns,
Weeping for this heavenly sign.

manna

What is it?
We wonder at
food fresh fallen
from heaven's pantry,
boring fare
for God's chosen.

Give us meat!
We cry aloud,
throats voicing groans
from stomachs grumbling
and longing
to be filled.

Let us feast!
We declare as
desert sands become
a banquet laid
with platters
of steaming meats.

Give us more!
Engorged dinner guests
demand, snatching and
storing too much though
the giving
Lord gave enough.

image

I saw a photo—
light snared in lens
and caged in pixels—
a face I knew years
ago.

It was the face of a friend—
a smile tangled in film,
laughter jailed by spool—
who's living look time
blurred.

But because of that picture—
memory and racing light
stilled to static frame—
I, bounding like photons, stand
still

and look

at an image—
day distilled to eternity
and sight saved for tomorrow—
concentrating a joy only
felt.

Lazarus

You would come
so often back then,
in our boyhood days.

Letters would herald
your visits, and I waited
at path's end—

seated under pine
and acacia branch—
praying you would see me.

When sun westered
below rolling ridges,
I'd see your silhouette, approaching—

haloed by twilight beams.
For endless hours, our laughter
crowned the Galilean hills,

lilting over fields
like summer's warm breeze—
you my brother from distant kin.

Will you come,
now, to your friend,
racked with fever?

Will you cool
the fire burning
to ash my once bright life?

I wait for you,
two days,
at my life's end—

laid beneath a silent sky
and dying light,
praying you will see me.

Yet no shadow
silhouettes the westering sun,
and I sink

to the grave.
Where are you, brother?

footprints

Are Galilee's shores
still printed with footsteps
where God walked with men?

Does sand keep
the shape of Him
who shaped its every grain?

Can earth hold
when heaven presses the
shore between seen and sightless?

Or

Does time
with wind and wave
smooth away where sacred walked?

Does the parade
of plodding wanderers
coming after obscure God's trail?

Will He tread
again the shores we
strode, imprinting our sands anew?

whisper

You haunt with hints
of delight—

that dance on the
tongue without material
flavor,

of music meeting the
ear without ever
stirring earthly
wind,

of light not born
of the sun lingering
on open
eyes—

joy,
the white space between
the lines of this story,
a whispered promise
of glory.

burn

When flame rages
and burns to ash
the oak and yew

whose shade, dappled
with tender light
and ruffled with breeze,

lulled me to tranquil
sleep and blessed
the July days,

what should I do
against the blaze
consuming my summer soul?

Should I douse what burns,
leaving damp sod
on drenched ground?

Should I rage against the conflagration,
anger rising like torching
tongues feeding the flame?

Or should I behold,
knowing who walks alongside,
and let the fire burn?

forsaken

Look to the Lord,
the Psalm declares.
Seek His face,
whispers your Word.

but

in Your command,
my question lingers.

Where are You?
my soul wonders.
Why are you hiding?
I simply ask.

for

in my questions,
the skies darken.

Will your hand unbind me?
I ask, a man besieged.
Is Your arm too short to save?
I wonder with palms slowly opening.

me

Your friend
You called me, a new name.
Daily bread
You broke with me, a free gift.

Around the campfire
We laughed, friends.
Under starlight
We talked, brothers.

Our songs
Filled the air, never desolate.
Our days
Lived together, never alone.

Yet

Laughter and song
Between us, I was empty.
Twilight talks and
Days together, I was alone.

Your loving gaze
I missed, seeing yet blind.
Your caring touch
I never felt, feeling yet numb.

My blank eyes
You saw, always seeing.
My lonely heart
You held, always gentle.

So

Like rain, the coins fell
Into my hand, arid earth.
30 droplets greased
My palm, betrayer's price.

The silver
had heft, real weight.
They lay
dense in hand, real mass.

But cold
were the coins, not Your warmth.
And heavy
was the silver, not Your light.

invitation

Cold, where heat has fled
Dark, where light has left
Still, where motion stops
Quiet, where noise fails

Can I overcome

Love, smothered
Day, darkened
Presence, stifled
Voice, silenced

heard

I raise a cry,
born of wound-
Is it reflex like
an animal trapped
in hunter's snare

or

is it the practiced
prayers of years
on repeat—
recited prayers to
a hollow heaven
echoing back pleas for
restoration?

Do my cries
come unto thee,
a suppliant's request
striving to earn
the King's ear?

or

do these prayers
die prostrate
kneeling before
an empty throne?

Is eternity the
absence of prayer answered,
silent chasm consuming
pious pleas?

or

does its commerce
resound with waves
of angel wings beating in concert
as their flocks fly to
lay at mercy's seat
the brittle jars
filled with my cries?

thrown

Simul justus et peccator

Am I just and sinner,
or just a sinner?

Is my sinning just,
or am I just sinning?

Like stones tossed
and skipping over water,

I cast questions,
awaiting the millisecond

where they, like your Spirit,
hover over waters

rippling with my
doubts and disbelief.

Yet let He who is
without sin

throw the first stone,
life in heaven's hand,

casting me, and every doubt,
on troubled waters,

trusting that You still
linger over the deep.

baptism

I yearn for a glass
and cool water to
fill the empty cup,

a drink I can hold
in hand and sip slowly
on a day un-paced.

But not always in dogma
or proposition my
fingers can grasp

do I find you
pouring the mystery
of yourself into

the tiny vessel
I offer cupped
in clenched hands.

Instead, you drain
the glass
running over with

agenda, presumption,
and narrow cares,
to render a chalice pure and

daring not to
confine yourself to
my cup,

You submerge me
in the mystery
of You,

drowning all I
hoped to know
and thought to hold.

fire

I long for Pentecost flame,
a blazing tongue articulating
praise thread by the crackle
of sacred letters, heaven-ward
syllables leaping like the Spirit
burning above my brow.

Yet in this quiet moment
when the wood has gone to ash
and the embers are a memory
of life once ablaze,
my tongue lies numb and
heavy in my mouth, a tomb
for worship without life.

But still you burn,
a small blaze set on candle,
a flickering light holding
vigil against the night,
for Pentecost fire is but
Noah's dove seeking
a steady wick to
hold its flame.

seeds

Seeds in soil
plunged deep by
grandpa's wrinkled hand,
the older digging
space and home
for life unsprouted.

On knees stained
with dust from
distant years and
wars in foreign
lands, he kneels,
honoring this earth.

I dug this
garden too, young
and unseeing of
the decades behind
his care for
young, unsprouted things.

Like the seeds
he sowed, he
sank into soil,
and I dug
this garden too,
burying another seed.

I pray his
seeds will bloom
in heaven's lands,
petals prophesying life
bursting from seeds
buried on earth.

sand

Cup your palm,
and scoop the shore.
Do you see the sand's grains,
coarse and dry,
fiery by day,
a mess already made?

And thus you are.

Fix your eyes,
watch the setting sun.
Do you see the sand's grains,
hungry for glory,
drinking twilight,
transfigured gold?

So you could be.

dance

What can you see in
these waters muddied by
doubt, despair, and desire?

Do you seek a
mirror beaming back
your holy face?

Is not this puddle woven
with dirt and earth just a
glass seen through darkly?

Yet when droplets jump
to air they catch
your formless light,

giving shape and
shimmer to glory
filling the sky.

Together, water and
light dance for
the moment they meet.

Are, then, these
waters meant to be
a mirror?

snow

Questions and doubts,
like late-December
snow, fall in
the night of
my soul's winter,

blanketing the lawn
I carefully kept,
blanching my verdant
pride so that
wandering eyes see

only the imprinted
tracks recording where
I wander in
all the concealed
queries my soul

would bury beneath
the soil of
manicured lawns and
hand-picked flowers
that bloom in
the spring of

my choosing, yet
you send the
snow to bury
my little garden
and paint white

the earth where
all can see

the tracks of
my plodding questions,
but when I

stop the pacing
and stand still
in the snow-
falling night, the
flakes absorb the

noise of yardwork,
busy highways and
voices clambering to
be heard, and
instead I listen
to the silence,

seeking and asking
for nothing but for
one who
would be still
in the stillness
winter snow gifts.

And there, where
earth stops stuttering,
heavy with what
I've laid down,
you crash out
of wood and
pine like a

deer, and on
that snowy night
in late December

our eyes meet
for a moment,
unspooling for a
second, lasting for
an eternity, and

I, surprised and
seen, dare not
blink or twitch
to savor the
unexpected moment of
meeting when hart

peers into quiet
heart, seeing past
silenced questions and
affirming me for
simply being there,

for grace is
the snow falling
over manicured lawn,
and joy is
the meeting made
true by a
man in silence.

About the Author

Chris Carter is the author of *Prodigal Disciples*, a devotional on the Gospel of Luke. He has also written for *Ekstasis Magazine*, *The Secret Place*, and *Bible Advocate*.